The Flight Cage

Rebecca Dunham

Confined, then, in cages like the feathered race,
they have nothing to do but plume themselves and
stalk with mock majesty from perch to perch.

Mary Wollstonecraft
A Vindication of the Rights of Woman

REBECCA
DUNHAM

POEMS

THE

FLIGHT

CAGE

Tupelo Press
North Adams, Massachusetts

Library of Congress Cataloging-in-Publication Data
Dunham, Rebecca
  The flight cage : poems / Rebecca Dunham. -- 1st pbk. ed.
      p. cm.
  Includes bibliographical references.
  ISBN-13: 978-1-932195-87-3 (pbk. : alk. paper)
  ISBN-10: 1-932195-87-4 (pbk. : alk paper)
  1. Women--Poetry. I. Title.
PS3604.U54F58 2010
811'.6--dc22
2010013906

Cover and text designed by Josef Beery. The typeface is Monotype Centaur.
Cover photograph: a crinoline cage (circa 1858) in the collection of The Costume Institute.
Photograph copyright The Metropolitan Museum of Art / Art Resource, New York.
Used with permission.
Back cover and page iii image: Sketch based on historic nineteenth-century crinoline.

First paperback edition: August 2010.
14 13 12 11 10   5 4 3 2 1

Printed in the United States.

Tupelo Press
P.O. Box 1767
243 Union Street, Eclipse Mill, Loft 305
North Adams, Massachusetts 01247
Telephone: (413) 664-9611 / Fax: (413) 664-9711
editor@tupelopress.org / www.tupelopress.org

Tupelo Press is an award-winning independent literary press that publishes fine fiction,
non-fiction, and poetry in books that are a joy to hold as well as read. Tupelo Press is
a registered 501(c)3 non-profit organization, and we rely on public support to carry out
our mission of publishing extraordinary work that may be outside the realm of the large
commercial publishers. Financial donations are welcome and are tax deductible.

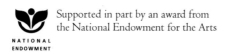
Supported in part by an award from
the National Endowment for the Arts

NATIONAL
ENDOWMENT
FOR THE ARTS

for Simon and Anna

CONTENTS

Séance

Notes

Acknowledgments

Mary Wollstonecraft in Flight

—London, 1795

So many rivers. Blood churning
through the veins, rain's

roped course down my wet
and unbound hair, the Thames' cold
body below. His forked

voice licked my mortal ears
clean. Men are strange machines.

He kisses like an ancient
God, his spit in my mouth a curse.
I can feel even now the heated
fury of his tongue and lips, how
they molded mine to his

design. The words I speak reduced
to birdsong and beating wing.

Cassandra's not the only
prophetess. I will not be confined,
content to peacock and preen

my manifold eyes. These storm-
soaked skirts will ballast
my fall, plumb as bridge pilings.

I have nothing
to fear from water's mean slap.

Let my lungs be coin heavy.
Let their two ruched pouches
swell pink and full as I sink, let

Putney Bridge be my final perch
and the October wind, my screech.

Terra Incognita

Women's psyche, of course, becomes an acknowledged
scientific enigma, like the inner substance of matter,
or the shape of the universe.

Barbara Ehrenreich and Deirdre English

Ergot Theory

—Ann Putnam in Salem, Massachusetts, 1692

It is a holy fire, this budding
body pricked and tingling. I set it
going with a single egg, henhouse-
hot, balanced atop my drinking
glass: a clutch in the belly

and I fall, convulsing, spine pressed
to unmade bed. Early snows
tangle tree and swampy meadow
like a sheet. *I desire to lie in its dust,
and earnestly beg,* a mongrel

bewitched by cake of rye and urine.
Through the kitchen, doctors
come and go, muttering that I'm
delusional. I pestle summer's sun-
baked kernels of rye to a meal.

This is the devil I have loosed,
its feet black and spurred as a cock's,
Rev. Parris claims, my vision
a mere blood-red globe of polished
fruit. I rock the grindstone back

and forth, either instrument of evil
or its victim. Back and forth, its
rhythm is the rhythm of a woman's
skirted body, tolling Gallows Hill
like a church bell clapper.

Flora Londinensis

— Mary Wollstonecraft from Bath, 1779

I am no invalid to be hung,
suspended amid steam and garbed
in brown like a wilting
champignon, and I am not Quality,

anointed with pomatum,
chalked face and hair achieving
architectural heights. I must be
like you, Fanny, or else

some new genus altogether
and sick for home. Paint me
meticulous, color-washed shade
of pistil and stamen outlined

in firm, accurate black. Linnaeus
knew even the wild flowers,
whether foxglove in Charlton-wood
or violet in a watery ditch,

must reproduce like men.
What I know is your hand, pressed
to mine. How it opened me
like a tender mouth, and gasping.

Terra Incognita

one: the harmonic body

> "In the harmonic body, the figure is constructed
> and expressed by geometry."
> —James Elkins

Beauty requires much. Flesh split beneath
geometry's blade, bisected breasts
fitted to divinity's grid. All projections
of the body distort it by pressing it flat—
Miss Helen Wills stares out of the page
in harmonic proportion, black and white,
her Peter Pan collar's scalloped edges neat
as her finger-waved cap of hair. Miss Wills
is passive, is patient, her flesh prepped
for the scalpel of a gaze. Thick lines ink
ratios and radiate from each deep-set
eye's soot bore. Her jaw curves, halved
like orange segments stripped from a fiery
globe. This face: a map of golden sections.

two: mappa mundi

A girl sits in lime-washed walls, asylum
window barred, one mat's slight rectangle
her only relief. O, hate. Its thin mercy
cushions hip and shoulder bone. Such care
deserves a *fuck you*, a body laid on hard tile.
Label the landmarks: Mt. Purgatory, Job
prostrate and erupting in a spill of boils,
or Lot's wife turned to cylinder of salt.
Pilloried, gypsum-soft: the past as both
cured and punishing. A single hemisphere
will suffice. Ocean rims the world and flows
round its back as wind whitecaps the disk's
shifting blue. She wants to hold its sea
in the palm of her hand, to be true center
to this solitude, surging like a continent,
lithospheric plate punching plate until
mountain ranges wrinkle up, until a new
white room opens its four-petaled bloom.

three: white

1. The point at which all narrative breaks.
2. Arthur Gordon Pym, afloat on Poe's
milky sea under a shower of ash. *3.* Of this
frontier, Captain Cook wrote: "its ice
extended beyond the reach of our sight,"
and that "the horizon was illuminated
by rays of light reflected from the ice to
a considerable height." *4.* The blank page
cartographers populate (whales and sea
monsters, legends unscrolling in cartouches
large as a country, and a single compass
rose petaled indigo, cochineal, and gold).
5. "The ultimate limit of a series of shades
of any color." *Syn.:* mute, meaningless,
implacable, dread. *Etymol.: n.* from point
of fear, *terra incognita* (past its pale curtain,
a giant the perfect white of snow rises up).

four: datum point

> "It is standard modern practice to relate
> excavations to a *datum point*, a fixed locus...
> that will not disappear through the years."
> —James Deetz

Winding into a layback spin, the skater
pumps her legs and frozen swags of reed
whip by; she rotates over the same
spot of ice: her head, shoulders, and spine
flower open, arms curving stamen-like,
right leg lifting, hips stretched wide
and heart served up, a girl getting her first
kiss—she holds as long as she can, spin
tracery unspooling loose as a careless
apple peel as she hauls in, gathering
herself, arms crossed over chest
like a body prepared for its final rest,
faster and faster, blurring until she breaks,
the world reeling white white white—

Aviary

Each day is a calculation: this
much from me, this much for him.

Like objects displayed in a hand-
thrown bowl, these words: *fig,*

pomegranate, lime. Grapevine,
crow, pineal, and *nib.* A still life

to press and test like any woman
at the market. It's really

not like that at all. The moon is
a smudge, a fingerprint on glass.

Its face phosphors the dark,
contained as the clock by my bed.

A *watch* is a nightingale flock,
sidereal song in the stand of pin-

oaks and olives. When do we stop
expecting to wake? *To calve*

can mean to splinter or to break,
to detach in a single piece. O

little box of mummified waves,
the body's surest form is loss.

Prison Box

Elaborate with compartments, its blue-
print shifts, movable partitions forming
and reforming in cells. *Always the same
shape, only very numerous*, Charlotte Perkins
Gilman wrote. There are always two of us.
The madwoman in the attic and the one
belowstairs, making pie, rolling out crust.
Blood stains the box's paper backing,
climbing and diving in a thicket of vine.
Her wrists flash fish-belly white, unfettered
as she lifts the crust then drapes it over
her glass pie pan, pretending the sound
she hears is just another chipmunk scrabbling
in the walls, a raccoon or ground squirrel,
best call up pest control, again. All the while,
her shadow body grows blue and cold
overhead, its difference tattooed like links
across the wild expanse of her skin.

Taking Leave

—Mary Wollstonecraft, January 1784

We sway in dimness, two dancers.
There's no going back, I say to Bess,

not now. The coach rolls along Church,
crossing the river and Meredith
by now must surely know we've flown.

Like a fury, Bess's hair, a plaited
and coiled nest of snakes — only pray,

let her shed this madness like a skin
that's grown too tight. Knuckle
to mouth she bites her wedding ring,

sighing for that *poor brat*
she's left behind. My fisted heart's

fierce heat beating wings
against its unforgiving cage. No words
for what he's done to her, save

the ones men give us. No way
for a man to rape his wife. *I cannot*

go back, she says. Then it is time
to switch the coach. By Hackney's
garden nursery, we rush from one

to the next. The smell of camellia, fern,
and rose filling the folds of our cloaks.

The Flight Cage

*—for Frank Baker, designer of the aviary
at the Louisiana Purchase Exposition*

His question was not the same one
Audubon once faced, no longer a matter
of arresting each avian species' distinct
plumage and light, but rather how
to frame a living piece of art, the heart's
allegro tremble as it pumps its wings,
how to display the beauty that is flight:
in 1904, it was the largest bird cage
ever built. Its elegant lines arcing,
the metal beams that strut and soar to sky.
What did he capture in the end, then:
the clumsy pink miracle by which even
a flamingo summons its body into air?
The human soul's answering upward leap?
Or the myriad ways that mankind's
ingenuity manages to bind the ineffable
to earth? The structure's steel trusses,
flying buttresses, arch up like a red-winged
blackbird in motion, muscles pulsing,
to form a cathedral more reminiscent
of flight than any of its inhabitants.

Mrs. Stevens

I sport a cap of wings.
1916's *Mercury* dime model, I am

collectible as anything of beauty
strikes him. Every room
just a compartment to house
his appetite's collection:

carved wooden figure of an old
god, Mandarin tea, a small
jade screen. Such a pleasure,
to seize an impression and lock it
up safe forever, he claims.

Scrawled paper slips, fetchings-
full, money his wallet.

But anything of beauty —
pungent oranges, green freedom
of the cockatoo — will turn to
witherlings left behind glass.

He treated his wife as if she were ash,
they say. *Witch,* they say.
Penelope-like, I wait

and enter each new day emptied
of the one before. Full moons
pressed like silver coins
to dawn's pewtered velvet.

Faith palls. Arms sunk
in the dishpan, my nights

are just another compartment
to house moonlight's fibrous
beams, woolen-white,

scraping me clean. I am
dour with dust, collectible as
anything of beauty. *He treated*
his wife as if she were ash.

I comb the powder from my hair.
Singing of walls, singing of ice.

Alfoxden

— Dorothy Wordsworth, 1798

Always we walk to, a great part of the way.
Wm. and I, hilltop to brook, and the sea
a morning basin full to its very lip. Turnip
greens lively and rough. The world in size
is but a tiny room whose edges we must
walk: Quantock, Holford, Stowey, Kilve.
Deft as I handle slips of plant, I find
of a sudden within me the gift to cluster
my thoughts until they twist, bristled
serpents dense as furze or hazel abloom,
midge-cloud in sunlight, or the oak
thick-feathered by scarlet-lit moss. Half-
dead, the sheep bell beds down for night
in a furrowed coombe's long hollow.
My journal pleases Wm., each day's entry
a small bud and I am glad. Its deckle-
edged leaves seem to me, at times, almost
to rattle between my pinched fingers like
the packets I empty over earth's harrowed
mound. My seed-black script smatters
the page. Leech-gatherer and night-piece
alike fly loose, words lifted and blown
by a wind, to fertilize some other's ground.

Migration

Two shoals of geese fly
low, mixing amid the cars
crossing Cedar River. Snow
sieves down and dark-
necked, the birds honk like
long-married couples
quarreling over which way
to go. I steer from
the place I was to the place
that I am going. *Migration:*
from the lost adjective
*migros, or moving.
Etymology explains me
to myself far better than
psychology. To my doctor,
I don't even try to explain,
I never do. The birds
sort things out and head
their separate ways, back
on course. Of course, I
know what I am: lost, home-
less, each abandoned self
rosaried and strung through
its vacant core. All night
this bothers me. One
point-bird must be wrong.

A Short Residence

*It is with some difficulty I adhere to my determination
of giving you my observations ... whilst warmed with the
impression they have made on me.*

Mary Wollstonecraft
*Letters Written During a Short Residence
in Sweden, Norway, and Denmark*

Brick and butter leaves thread
the breeze that banners our side porch,
picking up speed. Chimes lift
their hollow throats in sonorous aria.
Confinement is so unpleasant—

the wind lashes and snaps the land's
back, lungs emptied across plains
shorn or riotous green alike. Such a long,
thick arm. It does not discriminate,
that much I can say. *Days of weariness*

have so exhausted my spirits and it is
always the same revelation, over and over,
a particle broken off from the grand
mass of mankind. After months of this
I finally see how my life must always be.

—*Letter 1*

Must I always be like this, a negative
plate in its voltaic cell, point of lowest
potential. I pull the current to and through
me. *The sphere of observation determines
the extent of the mind.* On X-rays

my bones beam white and that is how
I know they run like char beneath my skin.
Don't talk to me of science. I will talk
as dark as I want and to myself or
pay someone to listen. I am not *afraid*

at the expense. Death is a subtraction.
It draws us, massing and flocked, iron
filings thick as the flesh-fly's larvae
on last fall's rodents. The ones we killed
into curls and left within our walls.

—*Letter 2*

Within these walls, our laundry fills
my arms. *In winter, they take*
the linen down to the river to wash it.
My mother should have hated
this chore, she did it so often.

Hands, cut by ice, cracked and bleeding.
White shirts lifted like snow geese
from her dryer. My father's arms made
young again, wrinkles in the crotch
of his pants erased and forgotten. *Men*

will not disgrace their manhood by
carrying a tub. This was forgiveness,
smooth hot iron in hand. But Mother,
knowing how not to burn the pale
cotton is not knowing how to love.

—*Letter 3*

To love is a thing one must be taught.
Just yesterday a few tight crocus
buds tipped through the mulch, mistaking
the year's last mild days for spring,
and today, ice sheets our yard. Thin

and burnt as cigarette paper, as ash,
the hosta's leaves disintegrate. *The severity*
of the long winter scorches: a new frost-
boil cracks the drive. The garden's unculled
tangle of cherry tomatoes dangle,

ever-red, brilliant gems on yellowed
vines. In the shed, burlap and fleece — *a fence*
to keep out the cold — go unused. We were
caught unaware. I toe the difficult earth.
Let us learn from this; let us take care.

—*Letter 4*

He no longer cares, I know. Though
there was a time when my lover
looked at wet clay and all he could see
was me, *the bones of the world waiting*
to be clothed. To rub two sticks together

and expect a spark is not a thing
to be counted on in need. *I saw the sun—*
and sighed. I pour myself a drink.
It warms me more than any fire ever
could. I cannot leave. My will

and words reduced like a dark, caramel
sauce upon the stove. *Shut the flue.*
How sweetly it smokes. *I left my little girl*
behind, mere stone and soil. Yet even
as a child I was intoxicated by pain.

—*Letter 5*

My child watches the salt pork sizzle.
A dozen potatoes fill the sink and I give
each its careful attentions, feeding dirt
to the drain. *Hapless woman! what a fate is thine!*
Years of scrubbing. Clay pots crowd

my kitchen shelves, unglazed and pink
as my daughter's skin, fresh from the tub.
Their contorted mouths beg to be
filled. *I dread to unfold her mind, lest*
it should render her unfit for the world she is

to inhabit. In the cove, fishermen land
for dinner. Hake and haddock pour from nets
like silver coins from a bag. Piles of bodies,
piles of pots. They gleam on the dock
like no human flesh, and ready for the broth.

—*Letter 6*

Mere human flesh, you
will sink, the water closing
neat as a wound overhead.
Where goes this breath? — this I,
so much alive? Sink,

until you forget the thick
green trees furring
the edges of your yard,
the churn of blood in your ears
loud as a river beating

the walls of some toothy
gorge. Sink into the swimming
pool liner's cloudless sky
and remember, to pass
the water test means death.

— *Letter 7*

The rainwater means death:
the fear of annihilation—the only thing
of which I have ever felt a dread.
It creeps beneath the walkout
door, soaking carpet, and so we turn

the air on. Blades spin and spark.
Then nothing—*only organised dust,*
chewed wires and a curled nest
of dead mice. Killed not by cold itself
but what followed: early melt

and an unknown hand to flip
a switch they never even knew existed.
I struggle to haul the rubber
tubes across our rivered yard, brace
my legs, and hose the unit out.

—*Letter 8*

Legs braced, the water's lip peels back from the boat's sides and we are
gloved in darkness. Salt pricks my bare shoulders and back, skin
seeds cascaded down just hours ago. My black dress dissolves
in the breeze. We are coiled, my groom's skin greening in globed
harbor lights. The smell of gasoline singes my nose as the mail boat

ferries us away, our figures standing, not touching, waving as night
blacks us out. Did the yellow lights of the pier bathe us gold
as the light when we took our vows, until death do us part, bird
seed spilling down our sides? Shadows fracture his features
and *the worm riots unchecked on the cheek of beauty*. My lips singe black and peel.

We could be any age, we could spend the rest of the night crossing
Casco Bay. Waves clap the boat's metal hull. I drop my gloves
like peelings among stacked sacks of mail, and the floor
beneath my sandaled feet vibrates. New rings coil on cool fingers
until death do us part. I do. The gold seeds pour down my body.

—*Letter 9*

Seed pearls halo the brooch,
set and pronged in place,
studding its oval slopes. Thin
sheets of nacre layer lustrous
paper over each minuscule

grain. *Ah! Let me be happy whilst
I can.* Death's fricative
hiss survives, helix-shelled.
*Wipe clear from my remembrance
the disappointments.* Prized

from the body's crypts
to adorn finger and throat
like a hex, it suspires, a jeweled
sea unseen, right beyond this
small room's open window.

—*Letter 10*

How an open window can catch
the face of Vermeer's girl,
its impossible angle, is his trick.
I know what that girl's letter
must say, how like a phantom

limb her body will remember his.
How *the world appeared a vast prison.*
I study the bowl of fruit, its apples
and peaches tipped to spill
in a study of abundance. She will

be a different woman by the time
she turns away, afternoon light searing
the wall behind her. Her reflection
will stay where it is, locked
in the window's grid, repeating.

—*Letter 11*

Against the window's panes, night
presses its panting body,
our house wedged in summer's
thick throat. All evening the lilacs
sag and whisper that my life

is a safe, its combination a cud
in my belly. Finger down my throat,
to me a sort of emancipation,
the blood gathers like a curious
storm. Save me from this

confinement which everywhere
struck me whilst sojourning amongst
the rocks, my past selves
all hanging about, muttering
the human body is only water.

—*Letter 12*

The human body is only water.
If not for the venous blue
twining it together, my body
might minnow away in a school
of slick and separate fish.

My uterus by now is swollen
large as a fist, the books
say. I float my hand's clenched
ball over my pelvis and recognize
the size of small violence

(the cloven foot of despotism)
used to describe my womb. Why
must it be anger's familiar
shape that helps us to conceive
the form and measure of our hearts?

—*Letter 13*

Heart-red and paper-thin, he
carves the roast. The tattoo of a rose
sways with my grandfather's arm,
another woman's name emblazoned
there. Grandmother's hands,

a steeple. The dead speak louder than
the living, she murmurs, God help us.
The world is still the world, and man the same
compound of weakness and folly. So
we eat, her orange pomander overhead.

Hundreds of cloves spike its bright
rind, as if punctuating each remembered
moment in her life. She rises to carry
meat back to the kitchen, its doorway
cool and dark as a sarcophagus.

—*Letter 14*

Cool and damp, March's
soil soaks denim and glove. I tend
my bulb garden — crocus,
hyacinth, tulip, narcissus —
beneath sky's blue vault.

On my knees, I free a tulip's
lance-like leaves, brushing
mulch's wet wood chips aside,
much as light drives the winter
back. Sun wakens the tender

shoots. They do not *bound*
over the dark speck of life to come but
spear up, thrusting death down.
Repeat after me, they seem to say:
crocus, hyacinth, tulip, narcissus.

—*Letter 15*

Crocus, hyacinth, tulip, narcissus.
Sprigs of violet and white. Lilac
spins in finger bowls filled with water.
The scent's warm pennies weight
my lids. Over the gravel drive,

purple bells cluster like hanging
grapes. The sides of cars marked by
winter's long spray of slush.
Voices rumble as if from a great
distance, *straying amidst a labyrinth*

of rocks without a clue, chanting.
They paint Grandmother's cold
body and rip the newly thawed earth
open. I pull my breath in. Barred
cage of rib locked into sternum.

—*Letter 16*

Rack of lamb: its barred cage breaks
white through the cold and purpled
meat. I bury garlic deep: dinner
for two. Her name, I say, I want you
to say her name. Then put her, please,

on a bus away from here, swiveling
on some bar stool in Chicago. *O jealous eye,*
she has been here first. He denies it,
blames the dehumidifier's static hum.
But we both know it's gathered beads

of her like a luke-warm wine for me
to drink. Outside, the azaleas explode blue
as her cotton shirt and heavy with her scent.
She drifts in through the kitchen window
to sit down beside us. An expected guest.

—*Letter 17*

An unexpected guest, my brother says,
our grandmother visits his dreams,
his door opening so a thin whip of light
snaps across the floor, unwinding
like a rattle snake as it strikes. All

I remember is the skirt of her swimsuit,
its shiny polyester petaled primrose.
Treading on live ashes, I am weary of how
her body *burned down to the socket* and sun's
white plate blistered sky. Her back to me,

she wades into the pool's shallow end.
Her suit's bright bloom skims the water,
hovering mosquito-like. For me, just
this cold water flat as a mirror and her back.
To me, she is always moving away.

—*Letter 18*

She is always moving away,
that other girl caught in the lake
glass, mouth creased by water's
tension. On one side of the dam,
it twists like a broken neck,

pooling warm and deep on the other.
To drink of the criminal's blood
is an infallible cure for the apoplexy.
This must be what it is like to die —
the last shovel of earth fallen

and my reflection finally pulled
back over my face, my mouth a cup
full of darkness, the dirt as soft
on my cheeks as light on a blind
child's face —   *Adieu.*

—*Letter 19*

I do not know how to open the fan
of this life and snap it shut tight. I want
the knots to all lynch fast enough,
someone to kiss me hard enough, deep
enough, and for good. Practiced as

a dancer, I know too well how to pivot
into the embrace, the smell of damp
peat and river water on that stranger
better than any mother's milk. *Listen
for the sound of my footsteps:* I've seen

the starlings scatter like dirt. I've heard
the stuttering of interference, a bad
connection, that garbled voice cutting in
and out like a bird in flight, the sense
of whose path can't be seen from below.

—*Letter 20*

This is a kind of sense, when
the sting of my fist makes me hit it
again, just so I don't have
to feel it. *Whether hospitals or work-*
houses are anywhere superintended

with sufficient humanity I have frequently
had reason to doubt. The doctors
insist: it's a pill or this shot, chemical
straitjacket, they can do it, can hold
me down. They tell me it's night,

shut my door, steal the lights. But
I have no windows, no way
to confirm the hands on the clock
stand true, that anything here is above
being bought, being subdued.

—*Letter 21*

Unsubdued as the season itself
they sprawl reek-wild. *But I,*
who received the cruellest
of disappointments last spring, desire
now the ramp's ovate leaves,

unfurling, *the grief, still fresh,*
that stunned as well as wounded me.
Skunk-cloud of onion and garlic laces
my breath. The same leeky taste
that threads the season's first milk

is tonic to cleanse the blood.
Credulous as a child, why have I not the same
happy thoughtlessness as their tiny
miracle, how they lift in utter
disorder from leaf-litter of forest floor.

—*Letter 22*

From leaf and litter, even in the winter,
the birds managed to thrive, moving
inland to the city dump. My father
tossed garbage bags into drifts of them,
forcing them skyward. They flurried up.

You will say I am growing bitter, perhaps
personal. But always, as we drove away,
I would watch them, white against
a gray mat of sky. I knew when we were
gone, the gulls would settle back

into abandoned mattresses and ripped
chair backs, to perch in dense rows
along mildewed arms. Scavengers, he said.
Our car bucked through frozen ruts.
Behind us they filled the sky like snow.

—*Letter 23*

They fill the sky, fireflies netting
the house and us inside it. *All*
the necessities of life are here extravagantly
dear. My son sleeps in his crib,
breathing. All day I teach him rules,

permanence. A spoon still exists
when it drops and people don't vanish
if they fall out of sight. But it feels
like a lie, *dishonourable as gambling,*
to promise him people return. It is

my own fear that makes his quiet form
a relief, right there where I left him.
It is magic. Lift the blanket
and he reappears: bottom up, legs
tucked beneath, genuflecting in sleep.

—*Letter 24*

Even in sleep defection haunts
this house, a dark swallow
perched in every overhead light.
She turns her cheek on the pillow's
cool linen — she's more than

half-gone — the crunch of snow
beneath tires in her ears. Not
a mile from this house the interstate
ribbons north. She's *determined*
to sail with the first fair wind.

And a pink-zippered robe, brown
along the hem, sits alone
at the kitchen table, an albino cat
threading and rethreading
the legs with transparent ties.

— Letter 25

Séance

We talked between the Rooms —
Until the Moss had reached our lips —
And covered up — Our names —

Emily Dickinson

Elegy for Mrs. Danvers

—after Rebecca *by Daphne du Maurier*

The end is always the same.
Caught in Manderley's gut, its frame
erupts about her iron form —
a living beast whose muscles shift
chinoiserie over embered skeleton.
Wind thrashes charred beams:
their carbon remains shiver to bright,
a carnelian poppy's petals in this

forged dawn. She could be any woman
immolated within the ruin of old
illusions but for her refusal to tolerate
our hero's daily betrayal, his lace
of lies. Vested in black, how I want
her face to be my mother's face.

Coulomb's Law

— *Mary Wollstonecraft in Lisbon, 1785*

I give the docks my back.
The river's surface is troubled,
a grave's muddy lid.

It's opened before as if on
a hinge, tsunami baring a floor
of lost cargo, of shipwreck.

Of 30-year-old bones. I know
you labor unfinished, flowing,
all sweat and tears. I'm coming.

Fissure and split, I will midwife
you, the heated charge
leaping from your skin to mine,

the cage of your chest flaring
hot as ruined *Convento de Carmo*'s
exposed and sun-fired arches.

Birth and death, it's all the same:
a difficult passion whose laws
flush the cheek and ruddy

the thigh. Like a forced bloom
you will sprout, Fanny Blood,
unfolding brilliant as your name.

Yellow

"Bless her little heart! She shall be as sick
as she pleases."
—Charlotte Perkins Gilman
"The Yellow Wallpaper"

1.

She looked like a precious doll, the mortician
said. Here in bed, I arrange my limbs
thusly, as if hinged. I will be
Incorruptible: body intact as the living,
as Maria Regina, dead at only 33
but exhumed four years later to no sign
of decay, wreathed and sweet as it smells
on high (though *faded by the slow-turning
sunlight*). Come winter, I will petal
the air a spray of daffodil. Yellow is
earth, orpiment, saffron and gold—most
holy metal. Coat my face with wax.
I refuse the journey forward, or back.

2.

They ply me full of fish oil, soft
capsules that leave my breath rank
as a cat's. My bedroom's leaded
windows wink honeycombed sun.
The color is repellent, almost revolting.
My son is not fooled by this form
on the bed, *he has no patience with faith*
and why should he? Just last evening
I dreamed I dropped him, the moon
a pearled egg rolling from night's
pouch, emptying its single sack.
I think that I am made for loss. And
when I found him at last, his face
was a perfect green mask of moss.
Earth takes back all that we neglect.
A comfort I am not ready to accept.

Reading a Biography of Akhmatova at 30,000 Feet

I drift amid ridges of cloud. *You won't be able*

    to remember much about me, little one. My young

son picks his way toward me below, I know,

    along some dark lash of road. Up here, though,

it is still light. Immense white masses swim past,

    whale-like. *I didn't scold you, I didn't hold you* —

the plane tips and all is blue, the small underbelly

    of a plane overhead, pitch as another boat's shadow

must seem to a sinking ship, there on water's

    far surface. Its black cross. *Motherhood is a bright*

torture, she said. Soon I'll rise from my seat, drag

    arms and legs through air heavy as water, and find

my son. *I was not worthy of it.* None of us are.

    We are made to resist. We fall, pressed as if

by an oaken slab, down through gray into night.

Confinement Ghazal

Like my great-aunt's crochet hook, it is plastic. Slipping
it in, the resident tugs and my legs flow slick with clay.

In 1797, the body opened itself to science. Men fingered
cadavers and sank wrists deep into birth canals, unclean.

Restrained and in pain, we are built for labor, petty
thieves straining amid our stained and russet bed-clothes.

Mary Wollstonecraft shivers in sepsis, shaking. Then the puppies
are on her, pulling milk from glutted breasts, eyes closed.

Crotch shaved, chloroformed, they strap my mother down,
slice her open, and pull me free, pinced in a metal claw.

Push, Rebecca. The doctor readies his knives and it is
as if the hand of God himself is there to set me screaming.

Séance

— Bess Wollstonecraft at Upton Castle

"I never think of our sister but in the light of
a friend who had been dead some years."
— Bess on sister Mary, 1792

Nought to be heard but the screech-owl
and you — what is it about castles and shades?

Poor Bess, I murmur to myself. I am
my only comfort. You think me weak,

hung suspended like a wilting fruit.
But you are no savior. My own child's

cold body, Sister, is ever at your feet. and
it is your hand, not a husband's, that

presses against my mouth until I wake,
gasping, night covering me like a grave's

muddy lid. So yes, I am restless.
Know that we sit down each dinner to

a dirty tablecloth on which repose
the remains of the dead. I have learned

much here, Sister. I can swallow hens
and cocks that die of diverse diseases — Nay,

can digest a dead mutton. *Poor Bess,*
I must even ask my employer's permission

to take a walk. No woman has a right
to what you have staked for yourself.

I give you my back, lost cargo,
a shipwreck. Your lips will not mold

mine to your design. Tendrils of hair vine
your neck. Like rope, I twist them

to whips in my fists. You refuse to see.
What I want is you, on your knees.

Encaged, as by God's Good Rage

—Sarah Good, 1692, to her daughter Dorcas and a nursing baby

I never set some broken knife's steel
blade to the afflicted, even as teal
tight, they flocked the pews, twisted eel-

like and crying. Milk daughters, I harbor
you, my own two yellow birds. Burr
my flesh, my familiars. Suck the meat or

sweat from between my fingers and spile
me. Dorcas Good, I forgive you your pile
of lies, the suckling snake you claim I

gave you, its flea-sized bite's red mark.
Listen, little nameless one. Do not arc
and squirm away. I am no more rock

for woman to pitch against woman
than witch or hag. Motherhood's an omen
that pricks and pinches, a needling in

the gut, drenching us all in blood-soaked
rags that we change in a privy's oak
dark shame, and oh, we are all afflicted.

Motets in Amber

Bring to me the two hot fingers.
Forehead and temple, they flash
over a cornfield's rows,
anesthetized and curared, all
dried stalks chopped
yellow sharp, stunted knives.

I'll convulse beneath the storm,
my body rubbed by
its woolen cloth to something
rich and new. Amber-bright,
I gown myself and go forth
frocked in feather, straw, and leaf.

If the past shines like a fixed
star reflected in the deepest well;
if its spring muddies his chill
feet, all wet and wildering; Thales
of Miletus will fall, felled by
a wild thirst down earth's pitch tube.

Amber: literally, burn stone. Or
in Arabic, *straw robber.* Dusky
birds hang like a handful
of ash thrown into air. *Electric:*
borrowed from the Greek

elektron, amber. Out our car's
window, I watch Illinois pour by,
power lines lashed to rich
soil. Moored as if by a wound's
stitched thread, its black cord.

The frog's dead muscles twitch,
kindled by jolts from Luigi Galvani's
electrostatic machine, proving
Thales of Miletus right: there is
no difference between the living
and the dead. Our nerves fire

and seek; what connects us burns
filament-bright, incandesces.
Resinous and vitreous in our glassy
vacuum, still we spark, charged
tungsten coiling. Why do I not
die? *Because there is no difference.*

My son traps fireflies in glass
jars, a constellation
to light his room, to flash
like semaphores across his sleep.

Nothing ends, or everything, if,
thunderbolt, you leave your cloud.

In daylight, their dull
amber bodies click
against the jar's clear neck.

Lamprey-like, lightning writhes,
June 1752, key knotted
to a silk string, *a continual stream*
the size of a Crow Quill, the bells
ring and ring, plasma and kite,
a slick flash, *a continued, dense,*
white stream whereby the whole staircase
was inlightened as by sunshine,
filling Leyden jars, the violet
corona of a ship's mast and rigging,
a blur no man can handfast.

Injured, my body exudes its
amber sap, planets fed to earth's soil,
its blue loam, a resin fossiled

lapidary fine. Only to be lifted
on ocean's current, *eel, torch, whip-*
lash, its long muscled arm, and foam
its way ashore. Set me aflame.
Aburn. Apine.

Oubliette

This is not a lament. My face
wears a mask I cannot lift.
Knock on it and it will sing: *you are*

born for boxes, soul threaded
through you like a wick wrapped
in wax. This is not a lament —

there's no nail that can split
its hull. Plaster-cast, it hardens
until I knock on it and it sings,

and it will not be shucked, some
borrowed dress, funereal
crepe, and this is not a lament,

though there is no sentry
to jump or kick, no castle guard
to knock about until he sings.

I speak through it and a voice
rises up and out, a thin wind.
This is not lament, but refrain.
Knock on it and it will sing.

Notes

The poems concerning Mary Wollstonecraft incorporate texture and detail that owe much to Lyndall Gordon's biography, *Vindication: A Life of Mary Wollstonecraft* (HarperCollins, 2005).

"Mary Wollstonecraft in Flight": This was Wollstonecraft's second suicide attempt, precipitated in part by Gilbert Imlay's infidelity and occurring shortly after her return from an extended business trip to Scandinavia.

Part One, Terra Incognita: The source of the quotation from Barbara Ehrenreich and Deirdre English is their book *For Her Own Good: Two Centuries of the Experts' Advice to Women* (Anchor/Doubleday, 1978; second edition: Anchor, 2005).

"Ergot Theory": See Linda R. Caporael's essay "Ergotism: The Satan Loosed in Salem," published in *Science* in April 1976. The italicized phrase is a quote from Ann Putnam, years later, when she apologized to the community for her role in the Salem witch trials. She was the only one of the so-called Afflicted to ever apologize.

"Flora Londinensis": As described by Lyndall Gordon in *Vindication*, her biography of Mary Wollstonecraft, Frances Blood's botanical drawings "were published by William Curtis in his *Flora Londinensis*," (16) the goal of which was to classify the indigenous plants of London's environs according to the new Linnaean system.

"Terra Incognita": The phrase "the harmonic body" is a response to the image "Harmonic analysis of the face of Miss Helen Wills" found in Matila Costiescu Ghyka's *The Geometry of Art and Life* (Sheed and Ward, 1962), plates 36 and 37. The James Elkins quotation is from his book *Pictures of the Body: Pain and Metamorphosis* (Stanford, 1999). The epigraph to "datum point" is from James Deetz's *In Small Things Forgotten: An Archaeology of Early American Life* (Anchor/Doubleday, 1977; revised and expanded edition: Anchor, 1998).

"Aviary": The phrase "box of mummified waves" was used to describe a Joseph Cornell shadow box.

"Taking Leave": From Gordon's *Vindication:* "In the eighteenth century Hackney was a centre for market gardening, with a nursery for ferns, camellias, and roses" (34). Mary Wollstonecraft's sister Bess suffered severe postpartum depression, and Mary and another sister, Everina Wollstonecraft, ultimately decided to assist Bess in fleeing her husband Meredith Bishop before he could commit her to a private madhouse indefinitely.

"The Flight Cage": Frank Baker's "Flight Cage" aviary, designed and built for the 1904 Louisiana Purchase Exposition, is now part of the Saint Louis Zoological Park.

"Alfoxden": Phrases from Dorothy Wordsworth's journal entries and poetry are recast within this poem.

"Mrs. Stevens": Elsie Viola Kachel (1886–1963), who was married to poet Wallace Stevens, served as the model for the Stevenses' New York City landlord, sculptor Adolph A. Weinman, and her profile appears in the design Weinman created for the 1916 "Mercury" dime.

Part Two, A Short Residence: The title, sequence, and many quotations in this series of poems are from Mary Wollstonecraft's 1796 work entitled *Letters written during a short residence in Sweden, Norway, and Denmark,* a very unconventional travel narrative divided into twenty-five "letters." The sources of italicized passages collaged here are the corresponding letters in Wollstonecraft's book, as indicated by the endnote of each poem.

Part Three, Séance: The quotation from Emily Dickinson is from the poem identified as number 448, "I died for beauty . . ." (circa 1862) as cited in *The Poems of Emily Dickinson: Variorum Edition*, edited by R.W. Franklin (Belknap/Harvard, 1998).

"Coulomb's Law": In 1785, Mary Wollstonecraft traveled to Lisbon to assist Fanny Blood with the delivery and care of her first child. Fanny Blood suffered from tuberculosis and died shortly after the birth.

"Yellow": Unattributed and italicized lines are from Charlotte Perkins Gilman's 1892 short story "The Yellow Wallpaper."

"Reading a Biography of Akhmatova at 30,000 Feet": See Roberta Reeder's biography *Anna Akhmatova: Poet and Prophet* (Picador, 1995) as well as Akhmatova's 1915 poem "Under an oaken slab ..." (translated by Stanley Kunitz and Max Hayward).

"Confinement Ghazal": Mary Wollstonecraft died of puerperal fever shortly after giving birth to her daughter Mary Godwin (later Mary Shelley). After the birth, the placenta did not detach. Lyndall Gordon describes the operation that was intended to save Wollstonecraft's life: "For the next four hours, Dr. Poignand tore out the placenta. He pulled it out in bits, torturing and resuscitating his patient, and almost certainly introducing an infection.... [Wollstonecraft] told [Godwin] afterwards she had not known before what pain was" (*Vindication*, 359). For fear her milk was contaminated, she was not allowed to nurse. "A bizarre solution was to put puppies to her breasts to draw off the milk" (360).

"Séance": Language in this poem is indebted to Lyndall
      Gordon's excerpts and analysis of letters written from Bess
      Wollstonecraft to her sister Everina (*Vindication*, 159–160).

"Encaged, as by God's Good Rage": Sarah Good was the first
      person convicted and hung on Gallows Hill for the crime
      of witchcraft in Salem, having been accused by young Ann
      Putnam, among others. She gave birth in prison, and her
      unnamed child died there. Her other daughter Dorcas was
      accused of witchcraft and was also an accuser, coerced into
      giving testimony against her mother. Dorcas was imprisoned
      throughout the length of the witch trials.

"Motets in Amber": Eugenio Montale's *Mottetti* were a formal
      inspiration for this poem. The italicized lines in section 2,
      5, and 7 are from Montale, translated by Jonathan Galassi.
      The italicized phrases in section 6 of this poem are from
      descriptions by Benjamin Franklin of his "lightning bells";
      see *The Papers of Benjamin Franklin* (Yale, 1962).

Acknowledgments

I would like to thank the editors of the following journals, in which these poems first appeared:

The Antioch Review: "Mrs. Stevens"

Borderlands: "Mary Wollstonecraft in Flight"

Crab Orchard Review: "Terra Incognita" and "Reading a Biography of Akhmatova at 30,000 Feet"

Cream City Review: "Legs braced, the water's lip peels back from the boats sides and we are..." (as "Night Ferry")

Elixir: "How an open window can catch..." (as part of "Trompe l'oeil")

FIELD: "Ergot Theory"

Gulf Coast: "Aviary"; "The Flight Cage"; and "Within these walls, our laundry fills..." (as "The Silver Saddle")

The Iowa Review: "Encaged, as by God's Good Rage" (as "Sarah Good, Imprisoned, 1692")

Jacaranda: "Rack of lamb: its barred cage breaks..." (as "Late Dinner, June")

The Journal: "Alfoxden"

Mid-American Review: "To love is a thing one must be taught...." (as "Letter to my Love on Autumn's First Hard Frost")

Notre Dame Review: "Elegy for Mrs. Danvers"; "Must I always be like this, a negative..." (as "Negative"); and "Yellow"

North American Review: "Oubliette"

Phoebe: "I do not know how to open the fan..." (as "Letter from My Brother") and "Seed pearls halo the brooch..." (as "End Note")

Prairie Schooner: "Migration " and "Motets in Amber"

The Southeast Review: "Prison Box"

Sycamore Review: "My child watches the salt pork sizzle...."
　　(as "Fish Chowder")

Valparaiso Poetry Review: "An unexpected guest, my brother says..."
　　(as "Letter-Elegy")

Vermont Literary Review: "Heart-red and paper-thin, he..."
　　(as "Sunday Dinner at Miller Avenue")

West Branch: "Confinement Ghazal"; "Coulomb's Law";
　　"Flora Londinensis"; and "Taking Leave"

I would like to thank Jeffrey Levine and Jim Schley for their hard
work and belief in this book, and also to thank Josef Beery for his
insights and the book's beautiful design. I was extremely fortunate
to begin this book during a fellowship at the Wisconsin Institute
for Creative Writing and to have been granted the time to finish
with the generous support of the National Endowment of the
Arts. I am indebted to my former professors for their guidance,
and to the careful attention Steve Gehrke, Colleen Abel, Emma
Aprile, and Kate Umans devoted to early drafts of these poems.
Most of all, I am grateful to Mark for his constant support and
willingness to read and reread poems, and for his understanding
that a change of punctuation is indeed an entirely new draft!

Other books from Tupelo Press

See our complete backlist at www.tupelopress.org